Ticking-clock quicksand

Written by Verity Croker
Illustrated by Andrea Da Rold

a Capstone company — publishers for children

Trent and I are hanging out in the sun on the sand. Bud, our dog, sees some gulls and starts to run.
Bud loves to run in the fresh air.
"Bud," I yell. "Come back here!"
He turns and stops, but he will not come back.
Then I see Bud start to sink into the sand. He is going deeper and deeper, and he keeps sinking. Soon, he has sunk down to the tops of his legs.
"Oh no! Quicksand!" I think. I jump up and run to Bud.
"Trent," I yell. "Come and help!"

Trent runs to join me.
"What shall we do, Emma?" says Trent.
"Grab my hand and do not let go,"
I tell him.
Trent looks at me. He will not like being hand in hand with me, but he loves Bud and can see he needs help. Now.
Like, right now.
We link hands. I creep along the sand. I put out my hand to grab Bud. But I am not as near as I need to be. I am afraid I will sink, too, if I go nearer.
"We need help," I tell Trent.
"I will go and get some," he says.

As I wait, Bud sinks further down in the quicksand. Now his tail is resting on the sand and I cannot see the tops of his legs at all.

I creep a bit nearer. I put out my hand as far as I can. But I cannot get to Bud. There is too much risk if I go nearer, so I wait.

"We will help you, Bud," I tell him.

Bud waits, too, fear oozing from him. Soon I hear yelling. It's Trent and Kim.

We all get down on the sand.
"Hang onto me," I tell Trent. "And you hang onto Trent, Kim."
Trent grabs me and Kim grabs Trent. I put out my hand, but the sand is getting softer. I cannot get near to Bud. He is so far off.
"Do not let go," I yell.
But it is no good. I cannot get to Bud. And the surf is getting bigger.
"Go and get help!" I hear Trent tell Kim. Kim runs off.

Trent and I sit with Bud.
Now Bud's tail is sinking under the quicksand. Bud lets out a soft bark as he looks at us. We hear a yell.
"Here we are!" It is Kim and Erin.
"Kim, grab Trent's legs," I tell her. "Erin, grab onto Kim."
"I do not like getting wet, Emma," says Erin. But she loves Bud and she will help us.
When Erin gets down on the sand, I see a black object slip out of her pocket.

"Can you ring for help? I do not think we can do this with just us," I tell her.
Erin nods, then rings Caz.
"Quick, Caz, quick!" says Erin. "And bring Fred."
Soon Caz and Fred are running up to us. We all get flat on the sand, Caz gripping Fred, Fred gripping Erin, Erin gripping Kim, Kim gripping Trent, and Trent gripping me tight. I inch nearer to Bud. I am near now, but I cannot get a grip on his short wet fur.

Bud is in the quicksand from his neck down now. And the surf keeps getting higher.

"It is no good," I sob. "We cannot get him out."

"Ring Linda," Trent tells Erin. "She is strong and smart."

"Linda," yells Erin. "Come and help us!"

As we wait, I tell Bud, "You need to be still. You must not sink deeper."
We all wait, still too, just looking at Bud.
"Here I am! I can help!" It is Linda, running up to us with a thick cord in her arms.
She hands the cord to me. "Put it under Bud," she says.
I get as near to Bud as I can.
"Yes! I can do this!" I think.
I dig in the quicksand and put the cord under Bud.

Then we all hang onto the thick cord. "Now pull as hard as you can!" I yell. We all pull. But Bud is still stuck. Trent drops his grip, but soon grabs back on. "Go and get Baxter, Linda! He is bigger and stronger than all of us," I yell.

"We must all pull as one to get Bud out," says Baxter, when he turns up with Linda.

We all nod and grab the cord tight. Linda and Baxter pick up the end of the cord.

"1, 2, 3, pull!" yells Baxter.

I feel a tug on the cord. I am pulled back a little.

"Keep pulling! 1, 2, 3, **pull**!" yells Baxter. With this big pull, Bud starts to shift in the quicksand!

I push some of the quicksand off Bud to help free him. Then I grip the cord tight and yell, "1, 2, 3, **pull**!"
We pull on the cord with all our might. We pull harder than ever. Then, Bud comes out of the quicksand! He tips onto me. I tip back on Trent, Trent tips on Kim, Kim tips on Erin, Erin tips on Fred, Fred tips on Caz, Caz tips on Linda, and Linda tips on Baxter.

We all get up, grinning and clapping our hands. I free Bud from Linda's cord and he jumps up on all of us in turn. He licks us, barks, and flicks us with his wet tail. What a good dog!